AF590818

Table of Contents

King Solomon

King David, my dad, ruled over Judah and the United Kingdom of Israel. After my father died, I then became ruler.

I know that I am wealthy and to show my wealth I am going to be the first to build the great Temple in Jerusalem which my father King David had dreamt about. When you enter the temple you will see the Ark of Covenant.

I myself ran into my wife's brothers when they asked to rent some land from me. Goodness knows that I had more than enough land and I told them they could rent the land from me. I never saw my wife to be until I had seen her working in the field.

Despite her background of not coming from a wealthy family and working in the field with her brothers, I immediately thought that she was a beautiful woman, but I did not want her to know how I felt at that time. Naturally, I love beautiful women and she is the most beautiful I have seen. We had a brief chat about work.

Here is the story of how King Solomon had put excitement into his relationship and it is never too late to put excitement into your relationship. The benefit of this book is to show romantic love for life, for pre-marital, marital, and post-marital relationship. Wild, passionate, romance and sex, is part of having a great marriage. Make this a priority in your relationship.

I Am Available To You

As soon as he left I thought to myself, why would Solomon propose to me? When I turned down his proposal I saw him walk away with his head down. I always thought with me being so young that I would not be ready to be his wife. I have heard others say, “You know that being married means, forever”. When I was lying in bed I was dreaming of the passion and desire I had for him. (See Song of Solomon 3:1-3) I had a nightmare that I would lose Solomon. When I woke up I thought about it Solomon did promise me gifts and money.

That was a sweet moment when Solomon proposed to me. I was hoping to run into him again. I could kick myself for turning down his proposal. My greatest fear is that I made a mistake. Well, it is morning and I am going to search for him because I have confidence that he would marry me.

Did I find him? Is he going to marry me? My husband to be I found and we then became engaged. Both of us believe that love is powerful and precious. I suspected he was up to something but I did not think he was going to throw a surprise engagement party for me. From time to time, my friends would come up to me and tell how happy they were for me.

The years had passed and her brothers had waited for this day, the day they had prepared their sister for her wedding day. They knew she had to save her body until her wedding day. She remembered her brother's words “Do not let your emotions control your behavior”. She thought, “Do not rush to have sex before marriage”.

(Proverbs 31:10-31) List the duties of a wife.

Excitement

(See Song of Solomon 5:10-15)

He was a chief among *ten thousand.* It was a bright day, when I saw my husband to be, this is what I noticed. He was handsome *white* and *ruddy. His hair is wavy and black as a raven.* His hands are strong and are of value like *gold rings* on

his fingers with *beryl* set in.

I can say one word, ***love.***

Love of his cheeks that are

sweet as flowers, noticing his

lips are like *lilies, dripping*

sweet smelling myrrh.

I can also say, he eases the

pain that I may have had

through the day when I see his

lovely *belly* that is as bright as

ivory overlaid with sapphires. I

find joy in the strength of his

legs as pillars of marble

Dear Diary,

My wife to be is so beautiful that she threw me off balance when I saw her. I have been waiting to look into her eyes which look like doves, they make me fill with happiness she will be my lover. Watch my great love I will make a house out of cedar for you.

It was a warm day, my wife to be told me that she was sick with love for the desire of me. She then, closed her eyes and fainted. I was able to give her some food to make her feel better. I took a deep breath I was mixed with emotions. She stood up and I was waiting to for her to embrace me.

Oh, How I Admire You

(See Song of Solomon 4:1-15)

Love is remembering how I felt
on our wedding day, seeing
your beauty! You caught my
attention on how fair and
beautiful you are! I was falling
in love I felt more love for you
when I saw you walking down
the aisle in the silver palace.

This was one of the most important events of my life. The clock was striking four and we were standing in front of the elders and witnesses. *Your eyes behind your veil* and I mean, how fair you looked. Your hair is so gorgeous, your teeth are magnificent, your lips are full, your neck is strong and your breasts are voluptuous. I have to restrain my desire for you.

Before daybreak my love, I will go to the mountain for you and get the myrrh and frankincense. My love, there is nothing wrong with you, not one blemish. Your love is so much better than wine I cannot wait to take you to bed! You will be satisfied.

You are like a garden full of spices. Now that we are married and home in my chambers, my love, the smell of those ointments and spices, I am going to rub the oils on you. You are so, attractive, I admire how much you have ravished my heart with those eyes of yours and that neck. I have the pleasure of the pleasant beauty of your sweet lips that are like honeycomb. Kiss passionately and taste the milk that is under my tongue.

My wife, you are going to have the best. Do you love the smell of my garments that are so divine? They smell of

Lebanon.

Dream or Reality

(See Song of Solomon 1:6&16)

Jada Watt:

What is it like being loved by

Solomon?

Solomon's Wife:

Dearest one let me tell you what is so great about him. First of all, everyone wants Solomon. To be explicit (See Song of Solomon 1:5) I am excited to say being a Shulammite woman black and beautiful too, the sun has darkened my skin. Just makes my love for him deeper.

My beloved is handsome he is mine and I have the energy that he wants. When he sees me he gets weak-kneed. Every morning he brings me a bouquet of lilies and he also feeds me amongst the lilies. He tells me that he loves me every day.

Jada Watt:

Have you lost interest for Solomon?

Solomon's Wife:

To answer your question I have not lost interest in Solomon. He sees me more beautiful every day. Do not stare at me because I am dark.

If you will excuse me now I am now going into the garden which smells like perfume to find my love.

Divine

(See Song of Solomon 1:2-4)

First of all you satisfy me all day. Being your wife I do not mean to be forward but I want you to come with me into our chambers and we will rejoice in each other, we will remember our lovemaking that is better than wine. My desire that is meant for you will always be in my heart.

Dearest

(See Song of Solomon 2:5)

Stay with me comfort me and

caress me because I am sick

with your love.

Dear Wife,

My loyal and faithful wife,

thou art beautiful, oh my love

you are a great delight to me.

True Love

Feet- He cares for them, which

will walk with you to Lebanon

Navel- He likes, like the lilies

Breast- Fruits

Neck-Chain

Lips-Kisses

Dear Diary,

(See Song of Solomon 8:14)

I have the benefit touching your body, of loving your feet they are so beautiful in your shoes. I smile when I think of your thighs that are like jewels, the works of a cunning workman. Navel is like a round goblet, belly is like wheat with lilies around it. My wife your breasts are voluptuous and strong neck. Your head is like caramel and the hair with purple ribbons; the king is held in the galleries. My passion is for you because you are so fair and pleasant.

You are picture perfect your stature is like a palm tree and your breasts are like clusters of grapes. I will climb up the palm tree and hold on to you. Her breast also reminds me of a cluster of vines and your nose smells like apples. She has the benefit of tasting the roof of my mouth which is like the best wine for her it goes down so sweetly that it makes me have sweet dreams of her and has me talking in my sleep.

The breasts that are just like my mothers are like the ones my brother used to suck. Her breasts are so irresistible that in time you will have yours sucked on. She is so special that it is going to be so good to you that she is going to want your breasts sucked on all of the time.

She is so beautiful I am going to have you drinking in bed. She is worthy of my spiced wine of the juice of my pomegranate. I will be hers always in our togetherness my left hand is going to be under her head. Her smell is so good to me my right hand is going to be tender with her and embracing her. I love him so much I do not want anyone to disturb him, sine I long to be with him forever.

Intimacy

(See Song of Solomon 7:10)

Solomon I noticed you watching me. Today is a refreshing day because I know that I belong to him and he wants me too.

Dear Solomon,

It meant a lot to me when I was told how beautiful I looked and knowing that you wanted me. I glanced at you also, you handsome man, you. I have prepared something special for you. It has been over half an hour since the last time I have seen you. Well, having a good man like you, there is

something special here for you

every day.

Love,

Your Wife

P.S.

I am so happy when you lie

between my breasts.

Solomon's Wife: We were sitting on the bed, when I asked Solomon about the virgins. I want to please know if the virgins love thee. He just leaned back and listened. I decided I would not ask him anymore. I just had lain back on the pillow and talked about me.

He is so handsome and I enjoy savoring his ointments in his chamber. He is so thoughtful he put honey and milk under his tongue for me.

Solomon's Wife: We were still in the bed when he put his hand behind his head and kissed me on my mouth. I began to lower myself in the bed to taste his love that is better than wine.

Setting the Mood: Before I came to his chamber I had planned everything in setting a mood.

The Romance: We were in the living room and I brought her into my chambers and I was glad and rejoiced in my wife. She appreciated the passion in the green bed. Her hot body was magnificent. I first touched her neck for it was smooth with chains of gold. She also told me the feel of my tongue was good and I know that she is committed to me. He is satisfied just let him sleep and let know one wake him up.

(Song of Solomon 3:1-3)

Solomon's Wife: Solomon and I were in the green bed. I fell asleep in the bed dreaming of Solomon. I could not figure it out Solomon was not next to me in the bed. I shook my head and wondered were Solomon was. I got out of the bed and stood up and thought he needs to be in this bed with me. I decided I have to go look for my husband. It is important to me to find him I just cannot seem to forget those kisses. You see, I miss Solomon, he is a good man, so I started running everywhere in the city streets looking for him. I was thinking will I find him? I feel that the watchman is not even helping me.

Solomon is gone. Has he changed his feelings for me because I did not want to have sex tonight? I am devoted to finding him, I found him past the watchman.

I held on to him and did not let him go. I enjoy being with him this is not a reoccurring dream. He knows he can trust me to take care of him, so I take him to my mother's house. The place I take him back to is the place where I was conceived. I will forgive him because I cherish him.

Solomon's Words of Wisdom:

1. ***Love Tips***

2. You have the desire to be romantic to each other

3. You are totally captivated by each other even if your bodies are not perfect

4. Long for affection of each other and has no desires of others.

5. Appreciate how each other effects one another to be better.

6. Trust each other/keep your personal business within the marriage.

7. Concern for each other/Say “I am sorry”.

8. Communicate on a daily basis and take each other seriously.

9. When you have a conflict with each other work it out.

10. Spend some recreational time with each other.

11. Be close with each other/nurture each other.

12. Be open with each other and problem a situation that may arise

13. Be understanding with other/Respect each other

14. Do not go to bed angry with each other

15. Pray with each other/ ask the Lord what he wants your relationship

to look like. Thank God for your mate.

16. Read the Bible together each night

17. Listen to each other

18. Eat dinner with each other

19. Passion for one another

20. Tell your wife she is beautiful/tell your husband he is handsome.

21. *Single-Ask the Lord what he wants your future relationship to look like.*

22. Have fun with each other

23. Find joy in being with each other.

24. Buy perfume/cologne.

25. Know where you could find each other.

26. Tell each other that the other one is special.

27. Give little gifts to each other.

28. Ask how each other day went.

29. Date each other.

30. Give a back rub with massage oils

31. Talk about what sexual pleasures you want from each other.

32. Have great sex!

33. Love is strong as

____

____

*Choose your battles carefully.

Romance = Stress Free

Marriage

For "Romance Me"

Workshops

Topics:

Learn practical how-to ideas for pre-marriage/married

1. **Romance your wife/Romance your husband**

2. **How to Love with your 5 senses**

3. **The Love of King Solomon**

Contact: elcelc.w@gmail.com

The Signature Christian

Space Singles

Dating Website

http://mysda7.com

www.ingramcontent.com/pod-product-compliance
Ingram Content Group UK Ltd.
Pitfield, Milton Keynes, MK11 3LW, UK
UKHW020217250726
13967UKWH00001B/51

9 781105 466816